Into Our Imaginations We Fall

Amy Howe

BookLeaf Publishing

India | USA | UK

Presentation by *BookLeaf Publishing*

Web: www.bookleafpub.com

E-mail: info@bookleafpub.com

ISBN: 9789357446303

First edition 2021

This book is dedicated to those who doubt
themselves and feel that they can't. You can.

Spring

Rise and shine little ones!
It's time to stop your sleep
And arise from the deep.
So chirp and scutter as you please,
While leaves return to the trees,
And clouds part for the sun.
It's time for a bit of fun!

Midnight's Big Adventure

Let me tell you a story.
Ups, downs and all its glory.
Bored in my cage,
I escaped! The world's a stage!
Naturally I must apologise
As this wasn't an evil demise.
It was a mistake you see,
But a rabbit's opportunity.

I ran through the streets and trees.
Definitely spoiled for leaves.
I arrive at a river.
Afraid. I start to shiver.
A dolphin pops from the water.
A kind smile you couldn't falter.
What a phenomenon!
"Name's Deli. Hop on."

I jumped onto her smooth skin,
Deli dived exposing her fin.
The elation I received
Was more you could believe.
The wind tickling my fur.
Suddenly, the river began to stir.

Into a tunnel, we landed.

A sewer! Your typical standard.
Yes it stunk! It was cold and dark.
Moving slowly, we hear a remark.
Somewhere deep in the abyss
An echo you couldn't miss.

A long sharp claw glistened in the spotlight.
Then two slicing eyes. A smile of delight.
Green slimy scales came into view,
Frozen in terror. We knew.

Tunnels whizzed past.
But the croc was too fast.
Abruptly we came to a halt.
A dead end. All in fault.
But a grate! Daylight above!
Deli threw me with a shove.

"Deli nooo!!!"
Silence engulfed the depths below.
Terrified, I looked around.
To my surprise was my surround.
My owner's home was right ahead.
I so wanted my bed.
Excited to see my owner once more.
I had never run away before.

What a roller-coaster I've had.
The good, the scary, the sad.

I did say "all its glory."
We've now come to the end of my story.
So give love to your pets and embrace
The gorgeous world in front of your face.

The Tree and the Door

I am a tree
And as you can see
I am completely free.

I am a door.
I stand on this floor.
Once I met a saw.

"A saw?!" The tree cried.
"Yes, it hurt" the door replied.
"The hunter was quite satisfied."

The tree welled up, he was sad.
"Oh no! This is bad.
"What about all the fun I've had?"

The door was in dismay.
"I'm sorry, tree. It has to be this way.
You have been led astray."

Life as a tree ended,
But as a door, he befriended.
They stood together, naturally a bit offended.

Tales of the Sea: Atlantic Storm

The galleon ship sailed gently along the seas.
Aqua green waters and the peaceful breeze.
The captain proudly watched his crew,
But alas, no one knew
That the prosperity and peace
Would soon cease.

Far in the distance
Was an impossible resistance.
Clouds darkening overhead,
The sea formulating a rocky black bed.
The Impending Doom's new find,
Slowly crept, the sailors still blind.

The sky rumbled.
The sailors looked ahead and crumbled
In fear. Danger was coming.
The ferocious waves crashed, drumming
Into the ship with all its might.
It was time to fight.

The captain looked down onto the deck
Screaming orders, veins in his neck.
Ship in full motion, everyone frantic.
The epic roller-coaster of the Atlantic.
The captain worried, but strong at his wheel.

The storm raged on, awaiting its meal.

The sailors ran, climbed, hoisted and all,
But this would be their downfall.
Sky swirling in blue, black and grey.
The monstrous waves towered it's prey.
The world got darker,
And it got harder.

Lightning struck in a flash.
These men were no match.
Panic, praying, abandoning ship
As a mast descended like a whip.
Watching as the ship split in two,
The captain had to accept he was through.

With little steps, he slowly walked.
Tears in his eyes, but not distraught.
"I did my duty and now I see,
It's time for the sea to take me."

In a Field of Roses

In a field of roses,
The sweet perfume that would fill your noses.
Hundreds surrounding the eyes to see,
Such a wonderful place to be.
A sea of green and red
Lies a place not many have fled.
This magical place of rarity
Brings love, beauty, peace and prosperity.

Not too long ago there was a storm,
Thunder, darkness, rain before the norm.
Yet as the sun revisits the skies,
The petals shine like fireflies
And calm winds rustle through the tranquility.
But if you have a strong hearing ability,
A whispering enchanting song proposes
The perfect escape in the field of roses.

Summer

Hip hip hooray!
Summer is here to stay!
Scorching sizzling in the sky.
Vibrant colours holding its light.
Playing together in their herds,
Animals fluster as they muster
For their freedom and delight.

The Caged Boy

There was an old man who lived in a shoe.
What a cruel thing to do!
Cruel you say?
Well, he had to pay
For a punishment to another soul
Deep down in a hole.

There was a little boy trapped in a cage,
Who screamed, cried, filled with rage.
The boy knew death was near.
Little boy? Death? Yes, that's something to fear.

Up above in the sky,
A winged creature flying high.
Black, gooey vile thing.
This isn't some fantasy fling.

The boy was dead meat.
He dropped to the floor, he was in defeat.
Please someone save the day
This boy's life can't go this way.

Remember the man who lived in the shoe?
Confined, punished, he knew what to do.
He ran and jumped onto the creature.
Ugly enough but he distorted its feature.

The winged thing howled and wailed.
Sword in hand, the creature impaled.
More strikes and it was run through,
Then the man and boy sailed away in a canoe.

Water

Placing your hand to the natural mirror.
Swish
Swoosh
Swish
Distorting your feature.
      Twisting
         Swirling
Patterns beholds.
Calming
Drip.
Drip.
Drip.
Soft tinkling of sound.
The perfect present is found.
Foamy white waves like galloping horses.
Stomps.
Beat.
Faster.
CRASH!
Into the sandy shore.
SPLASH!
Down into the depths you go.
Little bubbles tickling
Pop.
Pop.
Pop.

Against your skin.
Giggling.
Gleaming.
You rise,
Sparkling in the sun of the deep blue skies.

Tales of the Sea II: The Hypnotised Clown

There once was a man named Landy,
Who was carefree every day,
And on his trek,
He wanted to check
If the horizon was far away.

There once was a man named Landy,
Who sailed in a ship,
And by the sea,
He saw me,
A mermaid taking a dip.

There once was a man named Landy,
Who was stunned by what he saw.
Enchanted
And planted
His face to the sea floor.

I am a mermaid named Milly.
Swimming in the gorgeous blue.
Exploring
And ignoring
My father's advice that came to be true.

Yes I am the mermaid named Milly,

Who was going her own way,
And on my dip,
I saw a ship
Coming from far away.

I am just a mermaid named Milly,
Who saw a man drown.
He jumped in
And didn't swim.
A hypnotised clown.

Air: Faded Memories

Life was Beauty
Bliss. Weightless.
The wind whistling
Whispering soft sounds.
Stunning ebony hair
Whipping,
Tangling.

Her strong large wings
Cascading behind.
How she loved them!
Terrific. Black. Soft
Swirling patterns
Sparkling in the sun.
Secure. Homely.
Her identity.
Her soul.

Her end.
Humans feared her,
Below they gathered
With bows, arrows, swords
She was shot down.
Falling
Falling.

Deep in London,
A girl was born
With ebony hair.
Her life was average.
An ordinary girl
Who would go to school
Socialise with friends
Fantasy was her fav,

She hated rollercoasters
Reason she never knew.
Fear of heights, falling
Feeling this tingle.
Something was missing.
Back muscles empty, heavy.
Her mind.
A wall.

Rebirthed in this world
With no memory
Misplaced.
Just fear.

What if your life
Isn't your first?
Faded memories
Warped into stories,
And so much more to your fears.
 Of course, how would you know?

Autumn

Autumn, Autumn, it's time for autumn.
When the leaves go swish and swash
And go plop into a puddle.
The animals prepare to hibernate,
Gathering the food with a crunch and a munch.
It's time for Lunch!

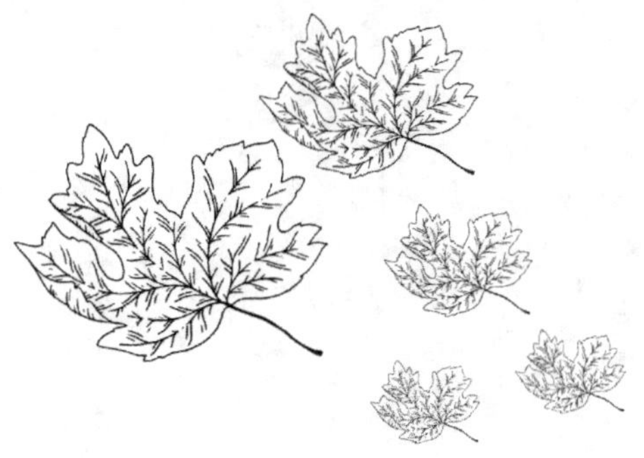

A Haunting Poem

Haunted houses are in movies and books,
They make you scream when you see their
looks.
Witches, ghouls, monsters and rats,
And sometimes, mysterious black cats.

In the story of this poem
Lies a haunting that's been ongoing,
With a gate, a castle and sign of BEWARE!
It's gothic design, but would you dare?

In the dark dark night,
I tread through the illuminated light.
The eerie glow of the shadowing moon
Hovers over the murky doom.

I pushed the door with a creak.
Tiptoeing, trying not to shriek.
The dusty darkness and all alone
chills me to the bone.

Someone is watching me,
Darkness engulfs. I can't see.
The rest is a blur.
Pain in my side begins to stir.

Excruciating. *Drip. Drip.*
Blood on the floor. I lose my grip.
Panicking, I stagger for the door
But fall to the floor.

What's that sound?
It's the howling of a hound.
I realise... I'm on Dracula's ground.

Hush

Hush little baby, don't you cry.
Mumma's not gonna let you die.
And if anything was to come,
It is me, having fun.

Hush little baby don't you weep.
Mumma's gonna let you sleep.
And as I creep, knife in hand,
Everything's gonna go just as planned.

Goodnight. Sweet dreams.

Fire

Licking the air,
The music sends high.
Dancing playfully,
Everything at peace.
Joy radiates
As they laugh and cheer,
Sending sparks
Into the night.

No one could believe
That this could be changed.
The innocence was pure.

Slowly creeping
From the inferno,
Comes the wrath
Of the beast.
The cracks and bangs.
Suffocation.
Mighty He
Engulfs his prey.

The Caged Boy - The Sequel

The hero of the story
Sat there watching in all his glory.
"This is the life I saved."
He was proud of how he behaved.

The boy's thoughts did not share.
He just sat there in a glare.
The man finally broke the ice
But of course this came with a price.

"I'm sorry for how things had to be.
I'm sure you must be angry with me."
The boy sighed and looked away
Muttering "should of let me stay."

"You did this!" shouted the boy.
"Don't make this a deceitful ploy!
You caged me! I hate you!
I'm hurt and scarred too!"

Everything was out of control.
The canoe reached a docking pole.
The boy stormed through the grass.
Guy chased but he was too fast.

Lurking within the green,

Two brown eyes watching the scene.
Sharpening his claws
And licking his jaws.

The lion pounced on the guy,
Pushed down, facing the sky.
The lion made a deafening roar.
The man knew what was in store.

The boy cried out to the man.
"Could it be I now give a damn?"
The child stared in horror.
Now he must be the stopper.

First he ran
Leaving the man.
The one he couldn't forgive,
But he knew that wasn't how to live.

He found a long stick
And started to pick.
Scrapping until his arms ache.
At last, he made a stake.

The lion was still on top of him.
The man's chances looked grim.
The lion exposed his vicious whites,
He was about to make his first bites.

Channelling his fright,
The boy jumped with all his might
And stabbed as hard as he could.
The lion was done for good.

The boy made a graceful land
And took the man by the hand.
He helped the guy to his feet,
Who was white as a sheet.

The man had distraught in his face.
"I was an absolute disgrace.
I was stupid and vile."
But the boy gave a little smile.
"I forgive you for what you've done."
Together, they walked into the setting sun.

Winter

Darkness looms over.
Sharp spikes swarm.
But twinkling stars fill the night.
Cosy cuddles with creamy hot cocoa.
Seeping through
The nestled nibbling keep,
Animals fall to sleep.

Set Yourself Free

The boulder pressed down on their chest.
Trapped in their own mess.
Heavy. Pushing into the ground.
Further and further, to be no longer found.

Cracks break and start to creak.
Bound up by their worries, unable to speak.
Ground opens to a second sky.
Falling, a permanent goal of fly.

Down and down into the dark.
Grasping, flailing, missing the mark.
Cascading into the Earth's core,
The burning abyss, they plummet to the floor.

Stretched and squished.
That freedom they missed.
They scream but no use down here.
Shivering and coated in fear.

Their eyes fill with tears.
Suddenly, a light appears
Down in their heart.
Has it been there since the start?

They begin to reminisce

That freedom they missed.
The joy, laughter and fun.
Their heart shined brighter than the sun.

Blinded, they stand on their feet.
Burning walls and no longer in defeat.
They blast through the mighty Earth,
Understanding now, time for rebirth.
Their life's purpose, they now foresee.
Finally, they are set free.

TiniTotts' Travels

This tiny TiniTotts was as tiny as can be,
But her smile swept the world with glee.
She wished to travel high and low,
But her size stopped her go.

It was raining one day,
She sat there trembling, wishing it away.
The raindrops falling and crashing,
Like giant bombs, thunder flashing.

The grey grass towering over.
The black sky trying to drown her.
This tiny TiniTotts was as tiny as can be.
"This can't be the end of me."

She stood up, standing strong,
Close to a new river, gushing along.
She wiped away the tears,
Concentrating, channelling her fears.

She picked up a leaf, bigger than she,
And rode the river, carefree.
The dark twisted rapid river,
But no longer did she shiver.

Faster and faster she went.

No longer would she live the torment.
The world cascading behind.
Adrenaline pumping, and a change of mind.

This tiny TiniTotts was as tiny as can be,
But her smile swept the world with glee.
She travelled the world high and low,
Not letting her size stop her go.

Piano

You press a key, it dings.
You hold another, it rings.
Press this, press that.
Will it be short? Will it be long?
Either way, you've made a song.

Left to right. Right to left.
Following the treble clef.
Hard soft. Grand true.
The crowd watches. The crowd is yours.
Claps and cheers fill the floors.

Joy of play, that's the life,
It slices anxiety with a knife.
Sigh of relief, you leave the stage.
Behold and wonder! I'll say:
My piano saves the day!

Sleep

I like sleep.
It's nice and deep.
You float away
At the end of the day.

The stars fill the night.
You turn off your light.
You snuggle cosily in bed
And bury your head.

Closing your eyes, you drift.
Time passes in a swift.
Dreams come.
Mosquitoes hum.
But you don't notice,
You're engulfed by the mist.

What is it that you dream?
Not everything is what it seems.
We see but don't feel.
You get a chill,
But it's not real.

Into our imaginations we fall.
Goodbadcrazy… You stall.
Sun shines, the night has passed.

You're ready to start the day at last.